Wa

Way of Resurrection

Jean-Pierre Prévost

NOVALIS

Introduction

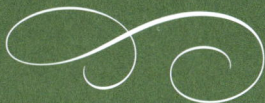

This meditation on the Way of the Cross is offered as part of the ongoing renewal of this devotion since the Second Vatican Council. Fewer people were embracing this traditional practice, whose fourteen stations were set in the fifteenth century, and the Church hoped to reverse that trend.

The renewal has taken place on two levels. First, the scenes featured in the Stations of the Cross are all taken from scripture – from the gospels. As we pray the Stations, our reflections are rooted in the Passion narratives themselves. Although traditional scenes such as Jesus' three falls and Veronica's wiping of Jesus' face, which are not found in scripture, have been set aside, this renewed Way of the Cross remains faithful to the narrative framework handed down by the tradition, and the story leads us from Jesus' condemnation to his burial.

Also, a fifteenth station is sometimes added, recalling Christ's resurrection and extending our meditation before a crucifix or an image of the risen Christ.

The Way of the Cross that I propose
in the following pages grows out of
both these aspects of renewal. Each
meditation is rooted in the four gospel
narratives that have been handed
down to us in the Bible: Matthew,
Mark, Luke and John. While the
Stations provided in this book do
not correspond to those traditionally
found in our churches, they may be
prayed anytime, anywhere, including
at church. All you need is this book.

The decision to introduce a station to mark Christ's resurrection was made to highlight this mystery, which, in the gospel narratives, is always presented as two sides of the same coin: Christ's death and resurrection. Without taking anything away from the merits of the traditional devotion, we must recognize that it focused exclusively on the Passion. And if there is one thing that the renewal in New Testament studies has revealed to us, it is the fundamental and foundational importance given to the proclamation of Christ's resurrection as the gospels were composed.

So the Way of the Cross that I offer
you here is not intended to replace
the traditional devotion – nor could it.
The number of stations has, however,
remained the same: fourteen. You
are invited to discover how best to
walk this Way of the Cross: at home;
outdoors, in a space that lends itself
to meditation; or in a church. For
each station, you will find

1. a gospel passage to be read silently;

2. a meditation on the gospel passage;

3. a reflection on a character or place
   in the scene described;

4. a personal prayer;

5. a prayer for the world.

May the crucified and risen Christ be
with you!

I. Jesus faces death alone

They went to a place called
Gethsemane ... and [Jesus] began
to be distressed and agitated. And he
said to them, "I am deeply grieved,
even to death; remain here, and keep
awake." (Mark 14:32-34)

Jesus can still find the strength to pray to the Father. But the heavens remain silent and Jesus' disciples are unable to stay awake. He faces death alone; he struggles against death alone. His prayer and his faith are enveloped in darkness. His heart trembles in fear. The Father's will becomes onerous, almost oppressive. This moment is heavy with sorrow and seems to be given over to the power of the prince of darkness. Yet Jesus continues to pray and his heart remains vigilant.

Gethsemane is no longer the garden of happier days, where the peasants' cries of joy could be heard as they harvested the fruit of the olive trees, and where Jesus so loved to pray. Gethsemane has become the garden of the most sinister of plots. In that garden, the worst betrayal and the most unjust arrest of all has taken place. The darkest of nights has fallen upon Gethsemane. The smell of death pervades everything. O Gethsemane, when will you become what you used to be – a garden of life and rejoicing?

Someday – will it be sooner or later?
– I also will face death alone.

Fear and anguish may overcome me.

But what if death did not come alone?

What if it was you, the man of
Gethsemane who was facing death,
who entered into agony once again

and came to offer me the comfort you
did not receive?

O Jesus, struggle with me and lead
me beyond death to new life.

Lord Jesus, you had compassion for fathers and mothers and you wept at the death of their child.

You wept with Martha and Mary at the death of your friend Lazarus.

But you yourself were alone, with no one to comfort you, as you faced the hour of your death.

Sustain those who die alone, abandoned by their families, those who are struck down by death without the chance to say goodbye, or who die alone, victims of violence or murder.

II. Jesus is betrayed by one of his own and arrested

Now the betrayer had given them a sign, saying, "The one I will kiss is the man; arrest him and lead him away under guard." (Mark 14:44)

What could have happened so that Judas, whom Jesus had chosen to be part of his inner circle, was now standing before Jesus to betray him and give him up to armed soldiers? Which of them had misjudged the other: Judas or Jesus? After being arrested by the soldiers, Jesus is handed over to the Jewish authorities, then to Pilate, and then back to the soldiers. How many human betrayals did it take for Jesus, the Just One, to be handed over to die?

"Traitor" is the less than flattering title that Judas has inherited. As if he was solely responsible for the terrible events of the Passion. Yes, he betrayed Jesus. He turned his back on three years of friendship and unforgettable moments spent with Jesus. Three years of learning from this teacher and bringer of the good news. But where were the other disciples during the Passion? Were they willing to be faithful to Jesus only when things were going well?

Lord Jesus, you have granted me the grace of your friendship, which you nourish by the gift of your Word and of your Bread of life.

I have discovered great joy in these gifts, Lord, and they have never failed me.

You alone know how often and how deeply I have betrayed you; you alone know my faults and my weaknesses.

O Lord of mercy, forgive me all my sins and bring me back into the grace of your friendship.

François Varillon, a French theologian, loved to say that we need to keep praying for people like Judas, and that we should never feel that they are beyond salvation.

Lord, you know that the human heart is complicated. You know that we can be blinded by the darkness. We pray that you shine the light of your salvation on Judas.

Use your power of salvation for his benefit, for he remains our brother, and for us, who have betrayed you in countless ways.

III. Jesus is judged by the religious authorities

Those who had arrested Jesus took him to Caiaphas the high priest …. Then the high priest tore his clothes and said, "He has blasphemed! Why do we still need witnesses?" … They answered, "He deserves death." (Matthew 26:57, 65-66)

Jesus will be condemned and put to death under Roman law. But above all he will die because of his way of seeing God and God's Kingdom, which troubled the Jewish leaders so much. They are all present: the High Priest, the scribes, the elders and all the Sanhedrin, including the Pharisees and Sadducees. Yet the trial is a travesty: his words are distorted, he is falsely accused of wanting to destroy the Temple, and everyone refuses to see in him the long-awaited Messiah.

The Jewish religious authorities are cast as the bad guys in Jesus' Passion. They are the ones who erred by failing to recognize the Christ, despite the many indications and signs. They read the Scriptures, they prayed the Psalms, they went to the Temple and the synagogues regularly. Was Jesus too near, too human, too free, too sensational? Is that why they brought accusations of blasphemy against God's chosen one?

I have often sought the approval and recognition of others, as if my own beliefs were not strong enough.

Lord Jesus, you always spoke freely and with conviction, empowered by the Word of the Father, and not by the approval of human beings.

Even when the teachers of Israel falsely accuse you, your words remain just and your silence is truth.

Lord Jesus, strengthen my lips, that my words and my life may always bear witness to you and your gospel.

Lord, why is it that there are more
and more religious groups and that
they fight among themselves to prove
which of them proclaims the truth
about you?

Lord, why is it that some religious
groups fan the flames of hatred,
all the while preaching peace,
reconciliation and love for others?

Lord, why is it that our prayers
and our places of worship remain
indifferent or powerless in the face of
cries of violence and rumours of war?

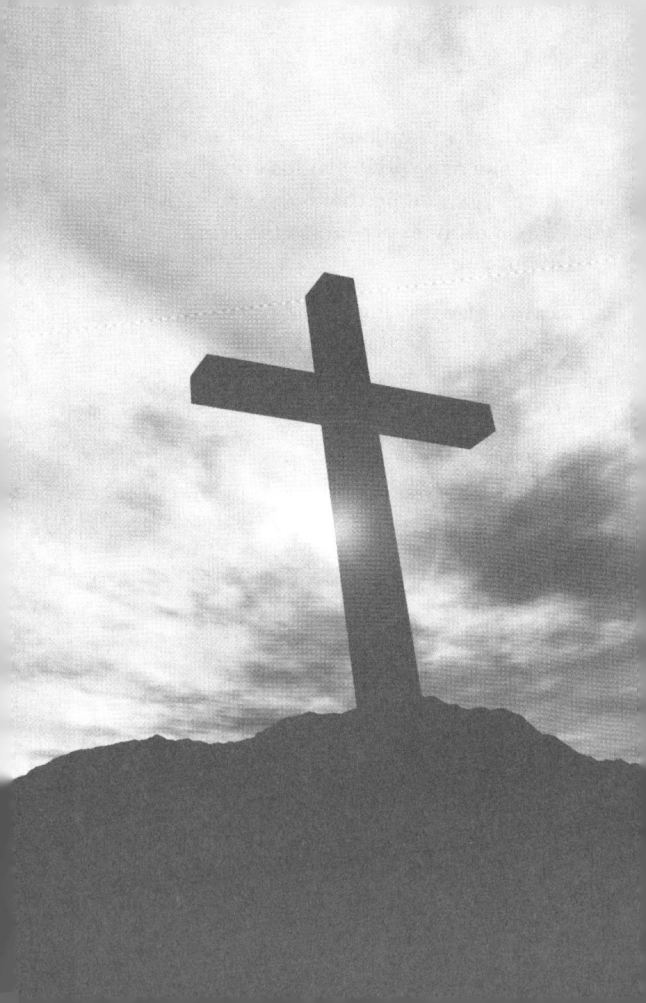

IV. Peter denies Jesus

Then [Peter] began to curse, and he swore an oath, "I do not know the man!" At that moment the cock crowed. Then Peter remembered what Jesus had said: "Before the cock crows, you will deny me three times." And he went out and wept bitterly. (Matthew 26:74-75)

For fear of being recognized, Peter hides in the crowd and follows Jesus from afar. At the first opportunity, Peter falters – not once, but twice – while speaking to a servant woman. Then, in the presence of many others, he denies everything about his time with Jesus: "I do not know the man!" What has become of his great confessions of faith? Who will weep the most? Peter, out of sorrow and repentance? Or Jesus, out of human kindness for Peter?

Whether he was called by the Hebrew *Cephas* or the Greek *Petros*, the meaning of Peter's name is the same: rock. Peter was always an authority figure. As Andrew's older brother, he seems to have been the head of the family fishing business. He was the first one Jesus chose among the Twelve, and Peter always took to heart the responsibility that Jesus had given him. During Jesus' earthly ministry and especially after Jesus' death, Peter acted as the true head of the fledgling Church.

His name was Simon. You called him Peter.

His faith reflected his new name: it was solid as a rock.

He had no equal when it came to professing that you were the Messiah and the Son of the living God.

In the face of a hostile crowd, he falters and becomes the vulnerable and fallible Simon once more.

You forgave him, and it was to "Simon, son of John" that, after Easter, you entrusted the mission of shoring up the faith of the disciples.

You chose Peter and his companions for their sincerity and their generosity.

You taught them the mysteries of the Kingdom, even though they might misunderstand or even rebuke you.

Your Good News took root in their hearts.

But these men remained human: fragile, fallible and sinful.

Lord, grant that your servants in the Church may be able to humbly and truly see themselves as fragile, fallible and sinful, so that, like the Church, we may rediscover the humility, freedom and daring that existed when the Church began.

V. Jesus is judged by Pilate

Pilate spoke to them again, "Then what do you wish me to do with the man you call the King of the Jews?" They shouted back, "Crucify him!" Pilate asked them, "Why, what evil has he done?" But they shouted all the more, "Crucify him!" So Pilate, wishing to satisfy the crowd, released Barabbas for them; and after flogging Jesus, he handed him over to be crucified. (Mark 15:12-15)

For Pilate and the crowd, who was more dangerous: Barabbas or Jesus? A rebel leader or a man preaching non-violence and mercy? Pilate sees no evil in Jesus and the crowd has stopped crying *hosanna*. All logic has now vanished. The accusation stems from a title that Jesus never claimed for himself and that held little or no meaning for the Jews. Persuaded by the chief priests, the crowd demands blood and forsakes all justice.

Except for Jesus and Mary, Pilate is the only historical figure who has found his way into the Creed: "I believe ... in Jesus Christ ... [who] suffered under Pontius Pilate." Pilate represented the Roman emperor in Judea – a tiny cog in the massive imperial machine. What's more, he was a ditherer and was blinded by the crowd's fury. During the greatest trial of history, this man fell pitifully short of his duty to uphold justice.

I am no one's representative and hold no political office.

I know nothing of power games and I blend into the crowd.

I am neither Pilate nor Caiaphas.

But all too often I may have washed my hands and lacked the courage to stand up for someone who was innocent.

O Jesus, you who have suffered because of our complicit silence, give us the strength to speak out against all injustice and to uphold justice as our only truth.

Today, there are many powerful people who wash their hands of the violence that occurs in their countries, of ethnic and religious conflicts, and of famines that wipe out entire populations.

Unmoved by even the most basic idea of justice, they hobnob with and listen to only the rich, caring only for their own wealth.

O Jesus, friend of the poor and of hungry crowds, transform the hearts of the powerful into hearts of compassion.

VI. Jesus is handed over to the soldiers, who mock and strike him

[A]fter flogging Jesus, [Pilate] handed him over to be crucified. … And [the soldiers] clothed him in a purple cloak; and after twisting some thorns into a crown, they put it on him. And they began saluting him, "Hail, King of the Jews!" They struck his head with a reed, spat upon him, and knelt down in homage to him. (Mark 15:15, 17-19)

The gospels provide very few details about the humiliation and torments that the guards inflicted upon Jesus. Humiliation and torture are a coward's form of justice. Torture of any kind is never justified, even for the most violent criminal. What about Jesus, then? This was a rushed trial. But they still found ways to mock and torture him: a crown of thorns, stripping him of his clothing, spitting on him, taunting him and, in the end, the ultimate disgrace, crucifying him.

The media often warn us that a news
report may contain disturbing images,
but then show those images over and
over again. A recent movie about
the Passion of Christ contained an
extended flagellation scene. Yet the
gospel narrative avoids describing
this event and does not even mention
the number of lashes the prisoner
received. The most shocking thing
is found elsewhere: in the parody
of homage paid to the "King of
the Jews."

I have never taken to the streets to protest, but I hate war and have no interest in military parades.

Why is it that we still haven't learned from the atrocities of past wars that the price we pay for using our weapons is always too high?

When will we ever learn that peace can only come about in a culture of peace, and not by glorifying the military?

There is no such thing as a clean war.
The atrocities inflicted on prisoners
of war violate every sense of decency
and humanity.

International conventions have
been signed, an international
Security Council has been created,
and charters of human rights and
freedoms have been approved.

But when we wage our senseless
wars, none of these laws or charters
can withstand the fighting.

O Jesus, you who were tortured
for no reason, you whose body was
humiliated, forgive the inhumanity
of all our wars.

VII. Jesus carries his cross

As they led [Jesus] away, they seized
a man, Simon of Cyrene, who was
coming from the country, and they
laid the cross on him, and made
him carry it behind Jesus. A great
number of the people followed
him, and among them were women
who were beating their breasts and
wailing for him. (Luke 23:26-27)

The cross is heavy. Even harder
to bear is the crowd's verbal abuse.
The road to Calvary is long.
Even longer is the agony of the one
carrying the cross, especially when
he knows he is innocent. Jesus
searches in vain for a friendly face.
Only a few women lament what is
happening, but they are powerless
before the crowd. Jesus tells them
to weep not for him, but for their
children and, by extension, for all
those who have chosen the path
of hatred rather than love.

It is a passerby, not a disciple, who is commandeered to carry the cross. The man was on his way home from his work in the fields and may never have heard of Jesus. None of those who were close to Jesus came forward to help him on the road to Calvary. There are probably many in this world who carry the cross of Christ, anonymously but courageously, hidden from the crowds and the cameras.

Today, I am again making this Way of the Cross that you once walked to bear the world's suffering.

I am reminded of all of today's crucified, whose bloody, mutilated and disfigured bodies are front and centre on our screens and in our newspapers.

O Jesus, you walked the path of the crucified in order to redeem all humanity's acts of violence.

Steady my feet on this difficult path so that, with your help, I can break down the walls of hatred.

VIII. Jesus dies on the cross

When it was noon, darkness came over the whole land until three in the afternoon. At three o'clock Jesus cried out with a loud voice, "Eloi, Eloi, lema sabachthani?" which means, "My God, my God, why have you forsaken me?" … Then Jesus gave a loud cry and breathed his last. (Mark 15:33-34, 37)

These last words of Jesus, taken from Psalm 22, form the most poignant cry ever uttered by any person. It is the cry of every crucified person. It proclaims all the suffering of the world. We hear other, more comforting words from Jesus on the cross. But none of those are more powerful than this call from the Son of God. It reveals total darkness, the darkness of all who have been abandoned. Will heaven hear this cry?

Tradition, especially in the realm of sacred music, has offered and continues to offer us many opportunities to meditate on these last words of Jesus. But more than any words can do, it is the cross that speaks to us; it is Jesus' death, his heart-rending cry that reveals his supreme love. Let us be silent: "Behold the wood of the cross, come let us adore!" Arms extended, head bowed, the Crucified One saves the world.

O Jesus, I gaze upon you on the cross.

How can I not be distraught and heartbroken?

You tirelessly preached the Good News; now you are powerless, unable to put your vast suffering into words.

You, the eternal and incarnated Word, must borrow the words of another to become the eternal and incarnated cry that carries our human suffering to the Father.

I can only remain silent and let your cry echo within me.

Lord Jesus, since you were a child, the psalms nourished your own prayer.

You sang and praised God, gave thanks to the Father, and shared the words of trust and joy of your people, Israel.

You also shared its words of sorrow and anguish.

From the cross, your cry carries to the Father the cries of all who suffer but no longer have the strength to pray.

Console them and let joy shine in their hearts.

IX. Jesus lies in the darkness of the tomb

They took the body of Jesus and wrapped it with the spices in linen cloths, according to the burial custom of the Jews. Now there was a garden in the place where he was crucified, and in the garden there was a new tomb in which no one had ever been laid. … [T]hey laid Jesus there. (John 19:40-42)

Jesus' companions offer their respect to his humiliated, bruised and now lifeless body. Two sympathizers ask the Roman authorities for his body so they can place it in a tomb that has never been used. For now, all is darkness and total silence. Jesus' body is held captive by death. While the soldiers cry victory, the disciples are afraid that everything is over. They believe that their hopes have been buried with Jesus' body.

One of these disciples was a member of the Jewish council, the other a "teacher of Israel." Joseph and Nicodemus are in good standing within the Jewish community, but both have "secretly" become disciples of Jesus. On this day, they reveal their secret and are not afraid to affirm their friendship with Jesus for all to see. When everything seemed to be over upon Jesus' death, we might suspect that they "secretly" harboured some hope, as slight as it may have been, that Jesus' story was not yet finished.

Lord, which of my family and my friends will still be with me when I set out for the afterlife?

Will my death come to them as a shock, or will they see it as a blessing after a long illness?

Will I leave behind some imprint, some legacy built upon my beliefs and my hopes?

Lord, you who have visited the valley of death, save me from the pit and lead me to the land of the living.

Lord, how many dead lie in pits of misfortune?

How many women and children who have been confined, assaulted and killed, and how many prisoners who have been tortured and coldly executed, have never known the final resting place of a tomb and have been denied their loved ones' final goodbyes?

O Jesus, Joseph and Nicodemus dared to come forward and claim your body. Have mercy on those whose bodies will never be found or claimed.

May they rest in peace as they are reunited with their loved ones, because of you.

X. Jesus is victorious over the tomb and over death

When the Sabbath was over, Mary Magdalene, and Mary the mother of James, and Salome bought spices, so that they might go and anoint him. And very early on the first day of the week, when the sun had risen, they went to the tomb. They had been saying to one another, "Who will roll away the stone for us from the entrance to the tomb?" When they looked up, they saw that the stone, which was very large, had already been rolled back. As they entered the tomb, they saw a young man, dressed in a white robe, sitting on the right side; and they were alarmed. But he said to them, "Do not be alarmed; you are looking for Jesus of Nazareth, who was crucified. He has been raised; he is not here. Look, there is the place they laid him." (Mark 16:1-6)

We did not have to wait for the apocryphal writings to learn of the key role that women, led by Mary Magdalene, played on Easter morning. They are the first at Jesus' tomb, the first to see it is empty. They are amazed and intrigued, but their very presence that morning points to an expectation that is beyond reason. Their hearts are open to receiving the first words of the Good News – "He is risen" – and passing those words on to the others.

The belief in an afterlife is an ancient one. It was shared by the Egyptians and the Greeks and came to the Jews later, around the third century BC. But Christ's resurrection goes beyond any and all of these beliefs. It is foundational to a new and innovative faith. When God raises Jesus from the dead, God inaugurates a radically new world, filled with promises of life and of a never-ending future.

I do not know how many of them there are, but I know the depth of their faith.

I do not know the secret, but I know the greatness of their love.

I do not know the reasons, but I know the strength of their hope.

I am speaking of the women who have helped me uncover your face, Lord Jesus: my mother, teachers, friends, religious women, married women who are involved in the Church, the woman who shares the daily burdens and joys of my life.

For them and with them, I bless you, Lord.

The Sabbath is something from the past.

The seventh day gives way to endless day.

Day of resurrection, day created by God.

It is a day of alleluia, of all the alleluias of the entire world, because Love has triumphed over death.

Love transfigures life.

Christ is alive, more than alive.

He is the seed of life for all and forever.

May our hymns acclaim him and our lives proclaim his love, which is stronger than death.

XI. The risen Christ appears to Mary Magdalene

When [Mary Magdalene] had said this, she turned around and saw Jesus standing there, but she did not know that it was Jesus. Jesus said to her, "Woman, why are you weeping? Whom are you looking for?" Supposing him to be the gardener, she said to him, "Sir, if you have carried him away, tell me where you have laid him, and I will take him away." Jesus said to her, "Mary!" She turned and said to him in Hebrew, "Rabbouni!" (which means Teacher). Jesus said to her, "Do not hold on to me, because I have not yet ascended to the Father." (John 20:14-17)

Mary Magdalene was not the sinner that so many painters have chosen to portray in their works; nor was she Jesus' wife, as some have claimed, although the gospels do not say so. She, along with other women, was Jesus' close friend and disciple. Her presence at the tomb is a sign of her affection and courage. There she finds not only her friend and beloved teacher, but the risen Christ, who sends her on a mission to proclaim the joyous news of Easter to his disciples.

The evangelists named her Mary
Magdalene to distinguish her from
the other Marys, including the
mother of Jesus and the sister of
Lazarus. Of all Jesus' disciples, man
or woman, it is Mary Magdalene's
name that is mentioned most often
in the Passion and resurrection
narratives. John even says that she
was there at the foot of the cross.
As the first person to arrive at the
empty tomb on Easter morning,
she has indeed earned the title of
"Apostle to the Apostles."

Hail Mary Magdalene, woman of
radiant faith.

Blessed are you among the disciples,
and blessed is your beloved teacher,
Jesus.

Holy Mary Magdalene,
present at the foot of the cross,
the first at Jesus' tomb,
set free by Jesus from your demons,
pray for me, a sinner,
now and at the hour of my death,
that the risen Christ will come to
meet me
and will call me, as he called you,
by name.

O Lord, how much longer must
we wait before women's voices are
allowed to evangelize our Church?

How many Mary Magdalenes will it
take before your Church, governed
by men, joyously consents to listen
to the voices of women, with no
restrictions?

Your resurrection has freed us, so
that there is no longer neither man
nor woman.

Lord, we await the day when we will
live in this freedom.

XII. The risen Christ appears to his disciples

When it was evening on that day, the first day of the week, and the doors of the house where the disciples had met were locked for fear of the Jews, Jesus came and stood among them and said, "Peace be with you." After he said this, he showed them his hands and his side. Then the disciples rejoiced when they saw the Lord. (John 20:19-20)

It took the disciples a long time to
believe, and they never understood
during Jesus' life what he meant
when he spoke of "rising from
the dead." Despite the women's
testimony, despite Peter and the
beloved disciple's visit to the empty
tomb, on that Easter evening the
disciples are in hiding and afraid.
The future is in question. Only Jesus'
presence in their midst can dispel
their fear and fill them with joy
once more.

It is already Easter evening and they have not left Jerusalem yet. They still have not seen Jesus again and the famous "third day" that he spoke of will soon be over. Judas, one of the group, is no longer with them. Peter still feels guilty about denying his Lord. And the other ten disciples are grieving the fact that they did nothing to help Jesus. As the risen Christ becomes present among them, they are speechless, but they sense a new peace settling within them.

I was always taught about the joy of Easter.

But Easter lasted for just one day.

Lent was long and filled with sacrifices.

Nothing compared to the solemnity of Holy Week: all four Passion narratives were read.

The Easter Vigil was wondrous, but it was Good Friday that attracted the crowds.

We had to wait for the biblical renewal and the Second Vatican Council to set the resurrection at the centre, and not the outer edges, of the proclaimed and lived Christian faith.

May the joy of Easter brighten each and every one of our days!

Lord Jesus, could it be that today
we are in the same state the disciples
were in on Easter evening: scared,
discouraged and plagued by guilt?

For a while, during the Council and
what followed it, we believed that we
would be reborn and that we would
carry the irresistible breath of the
resurrection to an anxious world
in need of hope.

O risen Christ, be with us.

Dispel our fears, dry our tears.

Grant us the peace and courage to
proclaim, as a renewed Church, your
resurrection, the promise of life for
the world.

XIII. The risen Christ commissions his disciples

Now the eleven disciples went to Galilee, to the mountain to which Jesus had directed them. When they saw him, they worshipped him; but some doubted. And Jesus came and said to them, "All authority in heaven and on earth has been given to me. Go therefore and make disciples of all nations, baptizing them in the name of the Father and of the Son and of the Holy Spirit, and teaching them to obey everything that I have commanded you. And remember, I am with you always, to the end of the age." (Matthew 28:16-20)

Even after the resurrection, the disciples have lingering doubts. Yet it is to them, fragile and fallible men, that Jesus entrusts a worldwide mission for all of history. Jesus wants to empower them with the same power of heaven that dwells in him. Although they had abandoned him, he does not abandon them.

This isn't the first time that Jesus sends his disciples on a mission. He has ensured that they are prepared and has given them specific instructions. In future, however, they will not be able to return to him to share their mission experiences; Jesus is about to leave them. They will have to find answers to problems that did not arise when Jesus was physically at their side. In the past, he had pointed out what needed to be done; now they will have to make their own decisions.

Lord, I am one of the privileged few who have had the opportunity to live in your land, to walk the shores of the Sea of Galilee, to read and meditate on your parables and teachings where you spoke and taught.

What a joy to imagine you in those places!

But today your land is torn apart.

Wars and colonization have built walls that separate people.

You wept over Jerusalem, and you weep today over this land where conflicts abound.

Change people's hearts so that peace may return to this land.

They are now back in Galilee, land of their youth, land that provided their livelihood.

It is a land that they travelled joyfully with you, Jesus, their beloved teacher.

They find themselves there with you for one last time, torn between faith and doubt.

But your words as their teacher are enough to send them out into the world: "Go therefore and make disciples...."

The whole world is now their homeland.

Wherever the Spirit leads them, you will be with them and in them.

XIV. The risen Christ sits at the right hand of God

Then he led them out as far as
Bethany, and, lifting up his hands,
he blessed them. While he was
blessing them, he withdrew from
them and was carried up into heaven.
And they worshipped him, and
returned to Jerusalem with great
joy; and they were continually in the
temple blessing God. (Luke 24:50-53)

The Gospel of Luke offers us a beautiful ending: Jesus' departure is marked by a blessing and great joy. The disciples will no longer hide behind locked doors, but will go openly to the Temple to praise God. In the Acts of the Apostles, Luke will revise this feeling of euphoria. The disciples will still have questions and will be tempted to gaze heavenward rather than face reality. The Spirit will make sure they are brought back to earth.

Ascension is the poor relation of the feasts of the Easter season. It lacks the radiance of Easter and the drama of Pentecost. It is also an enormous challenge for preachers: Who has been to heaven to speak about it? How can one explain the expression "sits at the right hand of the Father"? Explanations will have to wait, because what we need now is people who witness and take action so that the resurrection may shine at the very heart of the world. It challenges each and every one of us who must keep both feet on the ground and witness to this Jesus who "ascended into heaven."

Lord, why do so many Christian groups want to emphasize fear when speaking of your second coming?

You who came in order that all "may have life, and have it abundantly," do not let our human divisions jeopardize the joy of your coming.

Your birth was a day of joy, your resurrection was a day of even greater joy, and your return will mark the beginning of unending joy.

Amid the cynicism and despair that paint a dark picture of the future, our only hope lies in your promise to return.

"Maranatha – Come, Lord Jesus!"

While the earth unleashes new furies, while humanity relentlessly consumes and destroys it, we cry out with all our hearts for the day when you will return, when God will make everything new: heaven, earth and all peoples reconciled forever.

"Maranatha – Come, Lord Jesus!"

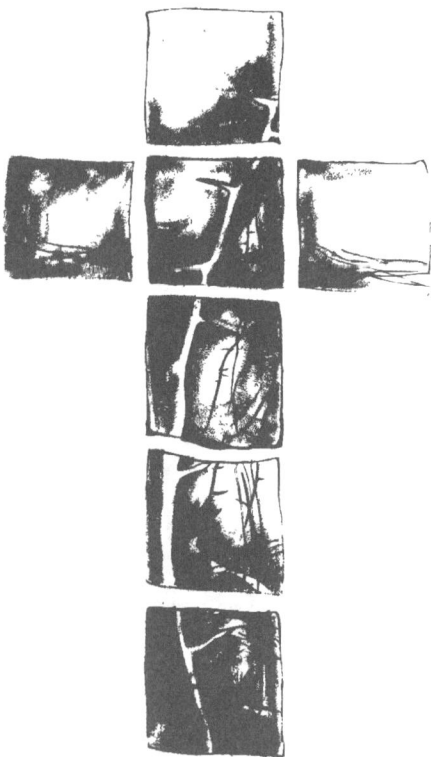

Conclusion

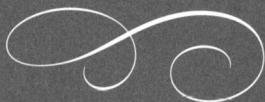

More than a simple devotion

The Way of the Cross is not just
another devotion. Its purpose is not
to stir our emotions, or to have us be
touched by the sufferings inflicted
upon Jesus. Rather, it aims to have
us participate fully in the events
that are at the source and the heart
of our faith: the Passion, death and
resurrection of Christ. It is not
about glorifying suffering, but about
becoming aware of Christ's great love
for the world, a love that transfigures
all our suffering and opens for us the
way to a new humanity.

The way to a new humanity

"Here is the man," Pilate said as he was about to deliver Jesus to the inhumanity of the cross. Yet no person had ever been as human as Jesus. Until the end, he assumed our human condition, and by giving his life for the world, he paved the way for a new humanity.

O Crucified One, disfigured man, transform us into witnesses and artisans of this new humanity.

Give us victory over evil and hatred.

Way of compassion

Christ's Passion is still happening today. Each and every day, a just person is arrested, condemned and executed for denouncing an injustice. Those who reject weapons as a means of imposing power are imprisoned. War is favoured over dialogue, apostles of peace are silenced, and regimes that flout human rights are supported.

O Just One, you who were denied all your rights, help us to confront hatred armed only with love and forgiveness.

Way of commitment

"If any want to become my followers, let them deny themselves and take up their cross and follow me." For Christians, there is nothing optional about the cross. It is not that we must chase after the cross or even impose a cross on ourselves. But we must each "take up our cross" and carry it rather than drag it along. There is no other way to be a Christian.

O Christ, you who carried your cross and ours, help us to recognize and share in the suffering of others.

O Jesus, the Living One and
the One who gives life,
O Jesus, the Sacrificed One
and the Glorified One,
O Jesus, man of suffering
and compassion,
open wide your arms to embrace
the world and breathe the peace of
your Spirit on all your children.

May the glory of your resurrection
shine upon us, and may the fire of
your love set the world ablaze to
destroy all vestiges of hatred and
reconcile all nations.

O Jesus, we gazed upon you in your Passion.

You, the risen Christ, who still walks amid your churches today, you come to meet us and knock at our door.

Enter, O risen Lord, consume our hearts with the fire of your Word and share with us your Bread of Life.

Walk with us today, guide us on paths of righteousness and justice, and rekindle in us the fervent anticipation of your Kingdom.

© 2013 Novalis Publishing Inc.

Cover design and layout: Audrey Wells
Cover photo: Crestock
Interior photos: © Shutterstock

Published by Novalis

Publishing Office
10 Lower Spadina Avenue, Suite 400
Toronto, Ontario, Canada
M5V 2Z2

Head Office
4475 Frontenac Street
Montréal, Québec, Canada
H2H 2S2

www.novalis.ca

Library and Archives Canada Cataloguing in Publication

Prévost, Jean-Pierre, 1947-
    Way of the cross, way of resurrection / by Jean-Pierre Prévost;
translated by Pierre Jacques LaViolette.
(Faith moments) Translation of: Chemin de croix, chemin de
résurrection. ISBN 978-2-89646-576-7

    1. Stations of the Cross--Meditations. 2. Jesus Christ--
Passion-- Meditations. I. LaViolette, Pierre Jacques, 1959- II. Title.
III. Series: Faith moments

BT431.3.P7313 2013   232.96   C2013-901685-6

Printed in Canada.

We acknowledge the financial support of the Government of Canada
through the Canada Book Fund for business development activities.

5   4   3   2   1   17   16   15   14   13